THE LAWS

OF

BROWN UNIVERSITY.

THE LAWS

OF

BROWN UNIVERSITY.

PROVIDENCE:
PRINTED BY ALBERT C. GREENE.
1851.

LAWS.

SECTION I.

SUPERINTENDENCE OF THE UNIVERSITY.

THE immediate superintendence of the University shall be committed to the President and nine members of the Corporation, to be elected from themselves by ballot, who shall be called the Executive Board of Brown University.

The President shall preside at the meetings of the Executive Board. The Board shall be so arranged that three members shall be elected at every annual meeting of the Corporation, each member being elected for three years.

The Executive Board shall choose a Chairman and Secretary, and keep in a permanent book, a record of all their proceedings; they shall meet, during term time, once in every month, and as much oftener as they may themselves direct, and they shall make a full report of their doings at every annual meeting of the Corporation.

It shall be the duty of the President to lay before the Executive Board at every monthly meeting, and as much oftener as they may direct, all such information in his possession respecting the condition of the Institution, as may enable them the better to correct what is wrong, supply what is deficient, elevate, to the utmost of their power, the moral and literary character of the Institution, and adapt it more and more perfectly to accomplish the design of its founders in establishing a school of liberal and Christian Education. For this purpose, also, every Professor shall present to the Executive Board a monthly report, exhibiting the amount of his labors in his department, the condition of his classes, and such other information as the Board may, from time to time, require, or he may desire to communicate.

It shall be the duty of the Executive Board to satisfy themselves that the laws of the Corporation are carried into effect by the officers, and obeyed by the students of the University; and to this end, they have power to enact and enforce every regulation required for the immediate good of the University, to call meetings of the Corporation, and, in general, to take such measures as may to them seem expedient for the well being of the Institution; provided always, that their acts shall be in force until the next meeting of the Corporation, and no longer, unless they be sanctioned by that authority.

Five members of the Executive Board shall constitute a quorum for the transaction of business.

SECTION II.

OF THE COURSES OF INSTRUCTION AND THE OFFICERS OF THE UNIVERSITY.

The following courses of instruction shall be given in the University. To them, however, others may, from time to time, be added, according to the pleasure of the Corporation:—

1. A course of instruction in the Latin Language and Literature.
2. A course of instruction in the Greek Language and Literature.
3. A course of instruction in Modern Languages.
4. A course of instruction in Mathematics.
5. A course of instruction in Natural Philosophy.
6. A course of instruction in Civil Engineering.
7. A course of instruction in Chemistry and Physiology.

8. A course of instruction in the English Language and Literature, and Rhetoric and Oratory.

9. A course of instruction in Moral and Intellectual Philosophy, and the Evidences of Christianity.

10. A course of instruction in History and Political Economy.

11. A course of instruction in Didactics, or the Theory and Practice of Teaching.

12. A course of instruction in the Application of Chemistry to the Arts.

13. A course of instruction in the Theory and Practice of Agriculture.

14. A Law School shall be established as soon as the funds of the Institution shall render it practicable.

The regular course of instruction in the Latin and Greek Languages shall extend through two years. It will be the duty of the Professors in this department not to confine themselves to grammatical analysis, but to advance to the higher principles of interpretation, and cultivate in the student a taste for classical beauty and an acquaintance with the phases of civilization, the modes of thought, and the leading political events to which these writings relate. They will teach authors as well as languages, stimulating the industry and directing the researches of the student in the field of ancient learning. Weekly exercises in written translation of the classics into English, or vice versa, will be demanded, and the Professor will specially require that every translation be correct in grammar and orthography, and strictly vernacular.

A third class, in either of the ancient languages, may be formed for such as desire it.

In the course of Modern Languages, French, German, Spanish and Italian shall be taught. In the early part of the course, it shall be the object of the Professor to communicate a critical knowledge of the language, in order to enable the student to use it as a means of investigation. As the course advances, instruction will be given in the literature of the language. Exercises in writing will form an essential part of the course of instruction. Unless by permission of the faculty, no student shall commence the study of a second modern language, until he has pursued for one year the study of that already commenced.

The regular course of Mathematics shall continue for two years, commencing with the elements of Geometry and Algebra, and proceeding to the more complicated relations of quantity. It is the design of the corporation that this study be so taught as to strengthen in the best manner the reasoning faculty of the student, cultivate the power of original demonstration, and render him familiar with the application of mathematical theorems to the practical business of life. For this purpose, original problems will be given out to the class during the whole of their mathematical course.

The course of Mathematics will embrace Geometry and Algebra; Trigonometry, plane and spherical, and its application to mensuration of heights and distances; Navigation and Surveying; and Plane and Practical Astronomy. Classes will be formed for the more advanced studies in Analytical Geometry, the Differential and Integral Calculus, Analytical Mechanics, and Physical Astronomy.

In the course of Natural Philosophy the laws of Physics will be illustrated and developed. It is intended that, in this course, the instruction shall not consist in a mere demonstration of the law, but be so conducted as to render an application of the law to the phenomena, and a reference of the phenomena to the law, habitual and easy. For this purpose all the necessary apparatus will be provided, and the student, as far as practicable, be accustomed to the use of it. The solution of problems will also be required, and it is expected that they will be of such a nature as to accustom him to associate these studies with the practical business of life.

The instruction in Civil Engineering will, for the present, be divided between the Professor of Mathematics and the Professor of Natural Philosophy. Its design is to prepare the student for those professions in which success depends essentially on an acquaintance with mathematical science. It is intended that it shall be accompanied by field labor, the examination of structures and machinery, and such attention to the solution of problems as shall enable the student in the best manner to reduce his theory to practice. Apparatus will be provided in order to enable the instructor to accomplish these results in the best possible manner.

The instruction in Natural Philosophy and Civil Engineering shall embrace the following subjects:—

Projections, and the principles of plane and perspective drawing; Experimental Lectures on Statics, Dynamics, Hydrostatics and Hydrodynamics, Pneumatics, Principles of sound and vibrations and Optics; on the theory and practice of Building, including wooden and stone buildings and bridges; the theory and practice of Mill work, including the elements and combinations of Machinery and the application of water power as a prime mover; the construction and theory of the Steam Engine; the construction of Canals, Aqueducts and Railways.

In the course of instruction in Chemistry, the Professor will be expected to unfold the laws of the science, and illustrate them by suitable experiments; to explain the relation of chemical laws to the various phenomena of nature, thus cultivating in the student those mental habits which shall lead him to observe and comprehend the changes which chemical agents are producing around him. Continual reference to this design will be had in the assignment of themes in this department.

In the course in Physiology it will be the design of the Professor to teach the classifications of the animal and vegetable kingdom, the most important modifications of organized structure, and the laws to which animal and vegetable life is subjected, with special reference to the subjects of health and regimen.

A private class will also be formed for instruction in practical chemistry, and also for original physiological research, under the immediate care of the Professor, for such students as desire it. For this course an additional fee will be required.

The course in English Language and Literature will embrace instruction in the formation of sentences, the cultivation of style, the construction of a discourse, the principles of criticism, and the history of the English language. The practice of writing shall be cultivated by means of essays, to be presented weekly. Exercises in public speaking, under the direction of the Professor of this department, shall be attended by the class every week.

The course in Intellectual Philosophy, shall embrace instruction in the nature and operation of the powers of the human mind, and the laws of their action, with the design of rendering the student familiar with the principles by which his faculties may be developed, and rendered more useful, in the discovery and dissemination of truth.

In the course in Moral Philosophy, the nature of the moral faculty and the laws by which it is governed shall be taught, and the duties of man to God, and those to his fellow-man, both civil, social and domestic, shall be explained and enforced. This subject shall not be taught merely as a system of abstract rules, but the Professor shall make it his object to eradicate error, inculcate ethical truth, and enforce moral obligation, and, by all the means in his power, strive to form the character of his pupils on the principles of the Christian Religion.

The course in History and Political Economy shall embrace instruction in the manner of prosecuting Historical Studies, followed by a view of the rise, progress, and present condition of the existing nations of modern Europe, with an illustration of the principles which have resulted in their various changes from prosperity to decline; the history of our own Government; and an exposition of the Constitution of the United States.

The course in Political Economy will explain the nature of national wealth, the laws of accumulation, and the principles by which national prosperity is governed, compare the economical institutions of different countries, and of the same country at different times, with an exposition of their effects upon the industrial progress of each, thus enabling the student to form for himself a correct opinion on those important subjects in this department, which force themselves upon the attention of an enlightened people.

The course in Didactics is designed, at present, especially for the benefit of teachers of common schools. There will be held two terms a year in this department of at least two months each. It shall be the duty of the Professor of Didactics to review with the class the studies taught in common schools, and then to explain the manner of communicating knowledge to others. The other professors in the University will be expected to deliver to this class such lectures in their several departments as may be desired by the Executive Board.

Application of Chemistry to the Arts. This course is designed for the benefit of those students who desire to engage in those practical arts, to the successful pursuit of which, a knowledge of chemistry is indispensable. It shall be the duty of the Professor to give instruction in the principles and practice of chemical analysis, so as to enable the student to prosecute investigations for himself. He will also explain the most important processes in the arts, exhibiting their defects, and suggesting the means by which they may be remedied, and keep his class informed of such improvements in the progress of the arts as come to the knowledge of the scientific world.

Course in Agriculture. This course shall embrace instruction in the principles and practice of agriculture, the natural history of the vegetables and animals commonly in use by the agriculturist; meteorology; the nature and treatment of soils; the management of the farm, and the cultivation of the most important products, both animal and vegetable. It shall be its object to enable the student to conduct the operations of agriculture upon scientific and economical principles, with special reference, however, to the soil and climate of this portion of the United States.

Professors shall be appointed for the purpose of conducting all the above named courses of instruction.

These several courses shall be so arranged in every respect as to accomplish, so far as possible, the following objects:—

1. To enable a student to pursue to the best advantage, any single course which he may choose.

2. To enable a student to pursue for a single term, a single year, or any other portion of time, such studies as he may believe to be for his advantage.

3. To allow students who are candidates for degrees to pursue the studies necessary for a degree in a longer or shorter time, as their age, ability or pecuniary circumstances may render convenient to themselves; the Faculty, however, having the right to direct the studies of such students in such manner as to prevent idleness on the one hand, or superficial haste on the other.

SECTION THIRD.

OF THE DUTIES OF PROFESSORS.

It is expected that every Professor will devote himself earnestly to the duties of his department, with which no other pursuit may interfere. Whenever the nature of the subject admits of it, the teaching will be by lecture and examination, with reference to text books and collateral authorities, accompanied by the writing of essays and exercises, and the solution of problems. It will be the duty of the Professor to illustrate every subject capable of visible illustration by diagrams and experiments; to direct his class to such authors as will be most useful in the prosecution of their studies, and examine them daily, not only in the lecture of the previous day, but in such portions of the book recommended as he may deem expedient. It shall be his object not only to communicate to them a given amount of knowledge, but to excite in them an ardent love of learning, and create in them both the desire and ability to prosecute their studies with interest and profit after their course of University instruction is completed. Each Professor will consider himself an officer of discipline as much as of instruction, charged with the special supervision of his own class. He will take notice of every instance of irregularity, absence or violations of the laws, whether in his own class or elsewhere, and take measures at once to correct it. If his own efforts be unsuccessful, or the offence is repeated, he will report it to the proper authority.

The exercises at each lecture shall continue for one hour and twenty minutes, unless otherwise directed by the Executive Board. Of this time twenty minutes, at least, shall be occupied in examination on the lecture of the proceeding day, and the reading which may then have been prescribed.

The times of lectures shall be so arranged that ten minutes of recreation may be allowed between the close of one and the commencement of another.

Every Professor, immediately after the daily examination of each student, shall record in his note book the numerical value of such examination. In the same book he shall record whatever demerit any student may have incurred for insufficiency of preparation, absence without sufficient excuse, disturbance, or culpable negligence during the time of lecture. These will all be entered upon his weekly report. No allowance is ever to be made for repeated negligence or habitual indolence.

The roll of the class shall be called at the commencement of every exercise, and a daily report of all absences shall be made to the President at 12 M., in which it shall be specified whether such absences are by permission, on account of sickness, excused, or without excuse.

On the Monday of every week, every officer shall make to the President a report of the standing of every student for the week preceding, in which shall be recorded the numerical average of his examinations for the week, together with the demerits which for every cause, except absence, he may have incurred.

The faculty shall meet weekly, at such hour as they may appoint. They shall choose a Secretary, and keep a permanent record of all their doings.

The President shall be a Professor, entitled to the salary, and responsible for the duties of that office. He shall be entitled to a salary in addition, as President of the Institution. He shall preside at the meetings of the Faculty, at which he shall be entitled to one vote as Professor, and a casting vote when the votes of the Faculty are equally divided. It shall be his duty to lay before the Faculty, all matters relating to the welfare of the institution which seem to him to require their attention.

The President shall be charged with the execution of the laws of the University, under the direction of the Executive Board. He shall have power to rule, govern and direct the University, and all matters relating thereto, and likewise all the students and resident graduates, according to the laws; and it is hereby provided that in all emergencies, the President shall have authority to adopt and execute, at his discretion such measures, not inconsistent with the charter, statutes and regulations of this institution, as he may deem expedient for securing the full benefit of the prescribed course of study, and the due exercise of discipline. He or such officer as he shall appoint to officiate in his absence, shall perform the religious services of the chapel. He shall matriculate every student who enters the University. He shall make a written report, once in every month, to the Board, of the condition of every department; and he shall offer any suggestions, and propose any measures, which, in his opinion, would tend to its improvement. He shall see that a regular and separate account is kept of the standing and character of every student; and he shall promptly dismiss every student, whose standing, either moral or literary, is such as to require dismission according to law.

Of the Remuneration of Officers. To each Professorship a salary shall be affixed, (as soon as practicable after the commencement of the present arrangements,) which shall be paid quarterly; and each Professor shall, in addition, receive the avails of the tickets for admission to his class, after deducting such incidental expenses as shall be charged by the Executive Board.

The price of the tickets of each class shall be fixed by the Corporation.

The necessary apparatus for illustration, as well as convenient rooms for the delivery of Lectures, shall be provided by the Corporation; but every Professor shall hold himself responsible for the condition of his lecture-room, and for the preservation and good order of the apparatus and instruments committed to his charge.

The Corporation have the authority to remove any officer, when, in their judgment, the good of the institution demands it; and also to appoint any person or persons of good moral character and ascertained competency, to teach in the University in any department of science or learning, whether such department be occupied by an incumbent or not, on such conditions as they may approve.

The emolument of no Professor shall be diminished except at six months previous notice; and no Professor shall resign without the permission of the Executive Board, except at the end of a term, and after having given two months previous notice of his intention to do so.

SECTION FOURTH.

OF STUDENTS.

Students of the University may be either candidates or not candidates for a degree. All however, shall be subject to the same laws, equally entitled to any certificate of standing which they may have deserved, and liable to the same punishments for transgression of the laws.

Opportunity shall also be offered to any person of good character, who may wish it, to purchase tickets and enjoy all the advantages of any separate course, under such regulations as the Executive Board may prescribe.

No student shall be admitted as a candidate for matriculation unless he bring suitable testimonials of good moral character; and, if he comes from another College or an Academy, he must also present a certificate of regular dismission and of good standing in the institution which he has left.

The earliest age at which it will be advantageous for a student to enter the University, is at the completion of the fifteenth year; the President is, however, authorized to matriculate a student at an earlier age, provided sufficient and peculiar reasons exist, and his parent or guardian places him under such moral supervision as is satisfactory to himself.

The form of matriculation is as follows:—A student who wishes to become a member of the University, must first present his testimonials to the President, who, if satisfied with his evidences of good character, will admit him as a candidate for examination, and direct him to the officers by whom he is to be examined for admission. If his examination be satisfactory, the student shall procure and read a copy of the Laws of the University, after which, he shall call again upon the President and sign a declaration of his deliberate intention to obey all the laws of the University so long as he shall remain a member of it. The President shall then give him a certificate of matriculation, which will entitle him to purchase his tickets, and proceed with the studies of his class.

As soon as a student is matriculated, the President shall send by mail to his parent or guardian, (if he be a minor,) a copy of the laws of the University.

A student, candidate for a degree, entering upon an advanced standing, shall be examined in all the studies which students of the same standing have previously pursued.

No student shall be admitted a candidate for the degree of Master of Arts, unless he sustain his examinations satisfactorily in Arithmetic and Algebra as far as Quadratic Equations, Ancient and Modern Geography, English Grammar, and the use of the English Language, and in the Latin and Greek Languages. He shall be able to translate and and analyze gramatically the Greek Reader, or an equivalent portion of some classical Greek Author; the Æneid of Virgil, Cæsar's Commentaries, and Six Orations of Cicero, or an equivalent amount of Latin, and be able to translate English into Latin and Greek. The object of the examination shall be to ascertain whether the student be well grounded in the ordinary branches of an English Education, and also, whether he be able to advance beyond the study of grammatical analysis, and direct his attention to the sentiments and course of thought of a classical author, and acquire a knowledge of the general principles of interpretation. Each Professor is the examiner in his own department, and is charged with the duty of seeing that these requirements are fulfilled. For entrance for the degree of A. B., the examinations shall be the same, except that the candidate need be examined only in the preparatory studies of that Ancient Language which he intends to pursue, if he elect to pursue only one.

Candidates for the degree of Bachelor of Philosophy, shall be examined in a similar manner in all the above studies, with the exception of the Ancient Languages and Ancient Geography.

Of Lectures and Examinations. Every student shall appear at the lecture-room of his class, punctually at the hour appointed, provided with a note book, pen and ink, and shall, without exception, take notes of every lecture delivered, as well as of the more important remarks made when the exercise is in part recitation. Deficiency in this respect shall be noted by the Professor.

There shall be three classes of Examinations for the students of the University. The first is the daily examination above mentioned, in connexion with the daily lecture. The second, is the examination at the close of each term; and the third, the examination for degrees.

The examination at the close of each term shall be conducted as follows:—

The Faculty shall appoint for the examination of each class, a committee consisting of the Professor of this class, and one other Professor, to whom the Executive Board shall add such other members as they please. The President shall, however, if he see fit, be excused from serving on the examination of any class except his own.

The Professor shall prepare in writing a list of questions to be proposed to his class at their examination, to each of which he shall assign a numerical value according to its relative difficulty. This list, thus prepared, shall be submitted to the committee for their approbation, and they shall appoint the time for the examination.

At the hour appointed, the students of the class to be examined shall take their places in the Lecture room, provided with pens, ink and paper. The written questions shall then for the first time be presented to them, and they shall be required to give their answers in writing, with their names subscribed, accompanied by a declaration from each that he has neither given nor received aid in the preparation of the papers presented.

When, in the judgment of the Committee, a sufficient time has been allowed for preparing the answers, the examination shall be closed and the papers handed in.

The Professor shall then prepare a report, in which he shall mark numerically, the value which he attaches to each answer, the highest number for any answer being that which had been fixed upon as the value of the corresponding question.

This report, when approved by the Committee, shall be laid before the Faculty, and together with the examination papers, shall be preserved in the archives of the University.

From this report, and the weekly reports of proficiency and conduct, the relative standing of all the students in each class shall be determined in the following manner. The weekly reports of the student in each study shall be added together. From this sum shall be deducted the demerits incurred in that study, and a proportionate amount of all other demerits. The remainder, divided by the number of his weeks of study, shall give the standing in each study by term reports. To this numerical standing shall be added the standing attained by the term examination, and this sum divided by two, shall be his standing in that study for the term. The standing attained in all his classes added together and divided by the number of classes attended, shall give the final standing for the term.

When this has been done, the whole class shall be arranged numerically. The maximum of attainment being fixed for scholarship and conduct, those students whose numbers amount to 75 per cent. of this maximum, shall comprise the first class of honor; those whose numbers amount to more than 50 and less than 75, per cent., shall form the second class; those whose numbers amount to more than 25 and less than 50 per cent., the third class; and those whose numbers amount to 25 per cent. and less, shall belong to the fourth class. All except those in the fourth class, shall be entitled to a certificate of proficiency, in which shall be stated the rank to which they have attained. If a student do not obtain a certificate of proficiency, his examination shall not entitle him to become a candidate for a degree, unless at the examination next following he obtain so high a rank in the same study, that the average of the two will raise him above the fourth class.

In preparing questions, conducting examinations and granting certificates, the Faculty will keep steadily in view the importance of making examinations real tests of scholarship, efficient means for distinguishing the meritorious from the undeserving, and for conferring honorable rank on young men of promising attainments and high moral character. It is the object of the Corporation, in these enactments, to render the testimonials and the degrees of this University, reliable evidence that the student has made honorable progress in the studies which he professes.

The rank which every student has attained, together with the account of his conduct, (if he be a minor,) shall be sent to his parent or guardian, at the close of every term, or oftener if he desire it.

A student, who without satisfactory excuse, shall absent

himself from any term examination, shall be entitled to no certificate and be liable to dismission at the pleasure of the Faculty.

Examination for Degrees. Candidates for degrees must have been entitled to certificates of proficiency in all the studies required for that degree. They will then be examined by written questions, either in the whole or in a part of the studies which they have pursued; and the principles by which their relative rank is to be graduated, shall be the same as those adopted in the term examinations. No student shall be entitled to a degree unless his attainment, on examination, amounts to at least 25 per cent. of the maximum previously established.

SECTION FIFTH.

OF DEGREES.

The regular Degrees conferred in this University shall be Bachelor of Arts, Bachelor of Philosophy, and Master of Arts.

The Degree of Bachelor of Arts is designed especially for those who desire to prepare themselves for the different professions, and yet, from unavoidable circumstances, are unable to pursue a complete course of liberal education. In order to render it accessible to such students, the number of studies is limited, and a large liberty of choice is granted, that they may be enabled to select such studies as will the better enable them to prepare themselves for a particular profession.

In order to become a candidate for the degree of A. B., the student having been regularly examined for entrance, must have been proficient in nine courses of one year each. Of these two must have been in an Ancient Language, one in Mathematics, one in English Language and Rhetoric, and the course in Moral Philosophy and the Evidences of Christianity.

For the remaining studies he may select from the regular courses such as he prefers.

The degree of Bachelor in Philosophy is designed for those students who are intended for the pursuits of active life. It is the wish of the Corporation to make the requirements for obtaining it, such as will confer a high degree of intellectual culture, without the necessity of studying the Ancient Languages.

For the degree of Bachelor of Philosophy, the candidate having entered by regular examination, must have been proficient in nine courses of one year each. Of these one must have been a Modern Language, one Mathematics, one English Literature, one History and Political Economy and Moral Philosophy and the Evidences of Christianity. The remaining studies required for this degree may be left to his own option.

A student who attends for two years the course of Mathematics, and the full course of Civil Engineering, may be admitted a candidate for the degree of Bachelor of Philosophy, by obtaining testimonials of proficiency in such other courses as shall, in the judgment of the Faculty, make his whole amount of study equal to nine courses of one year each. The same principle shall also be applied to students who pursue either of the other special courses.

The candidates for these degrees will then be examined in the manner above specified, in three of the studies in which they have been proficients. The studies in which the examinations will be held, will be made known to the University at the beginning of the term immediately preceding the Commencement.

The degree of Master of Arts is intended for those students who desire to pursue a full course of liberal education. In order to become a candidate for this degree, the student must have obtained certificates of proficiency in the following courses of instruction:—

In the Ancient Languages for two years,

In one Modern Language for one year,

In the Mathematics of two years,

In Natural Philosophy,

English Language and Rhetoric,

Chemistry and Physiology,

History and Political Economy,

Intellectual and Moral Philosophy, and the Evidences of Christianity.

He must also be examined in the Ancient Languages, in Natural Philosophy, and in three other studies of the course, to be selected by the Faculty; and he shall not be entitled to a degree unless his answers attain to 25 per cent. of the maximum established by the Faculty. The examination in the Ancient Languages shall include one author in Latin and one in Greek, which has not been read by the class in the regular course of instruction.

The candidate for this degree may be allowed to substitute a third year in an Ancient Language for a second in Mathematics, or a third year in Mathematics, for a second in an Ancient Language; or to substitute one Modern Language for a year in an Ancient Language, or for a year in Mathematics.

It is the design of the Corporation to require for the degree of Bachelor of Arts and of Philosophy, an amount of study which *may* be accomplished in three years, but which may, if he pleases, occupy the student profitably for four years; and to require for the degree of Master of Arts an amount of study which *may* be accomplished in four years, but which, if generously pursued, may occupy the student with advantage a considerable longer time. And the Faculty have the power to direct in all cases the discontinuance of a third study, or the addition of a third to two already pursued, if such diminution or addition of labor will, in their opinion, be for the advantage of the student. Whenever a study is thus postponed, the ticket which the student has purchased shall be available for the same course at any subsequent time without additional charge.

The questions in the examination for degrees shall be published in the following annual catalogue of the University.

Degrees of A. M. in course shall not be conferred in this University, on students who enter after the annual commencement of the year 1850.

SECTION SIXTH.

OF DISCIPLINE.

The principles which are intended to control the discipline of this institution, are the following :—

1. The Corporation enact such laws as they believe adapted to promote the ends for which a University is established, namely, the moral and intellectual improvement of the young gentlemen who may be committed to their charge.

2. Every student who becomes a member of the University has been required to read the laws, and he has deliberately promised to obey them.

3. Every parent or guardian, (if the student be a minor,) is also furnished with a copy of the laws, so that, if he do not approve of them, he may withdraw the student under his charge immediately.

4. These conditions being mutually understood, and any student being at liberty at any time to withdraw, with all the testimonials of standing and character to which he is entitled; if they are repeatedly or deliberately violated, the relation between the parties must cease by the dismission of the student. And, moreover, an institution of learning being designed for the purpose of affording intellectual and moral culture to those who desire to avail themselves of its advantages, it can never be made the resort of the idle, the negligent, and the dissolute. A system of discipline should therefore be adopted for such an institution, which will, after a sufficient trial, inevitably lead to the dismission of those whose residence can be of no benefit, either to themselves or to the University.

In order to accomplish the above objects, the following regulations are established :—

Immediately after the daily examination of each student, the Professor shall affix a numerical mark to his name, designating the value of his examination. For a perfect recitation the number shall be 20, for a less perfect one a smaller number, and for a deficiency, 0.

If the deficiency have been satisfactory explained before the commencement of the lecture, that is, if it have arisen from circumstances over which the student had no control, no other mark shall be added. If the explanation be unsatisfactory, or if no explanation be offered, it shall incur an additional mark of *demerit* of from 5 to 20. Disturbance in chapel, or in lecture room, or in any part of the college premises, shall incur a demerit of from 5 to 20.

Absence from lecture at the time of calling the roll, unless previous permission be given, or unless the reason why such permission could not be requested be rendered previously to 12 o'clock M., of the subsequent day, shall incur a demerit of from 5 to 20. Absence from rooms after dark, and before 9 o'clock, P. M., a demerit of 10; if after 9 P. M., a demerit of 20.

Intemperance, licentiousness, profanity, or any conduct which renders a student an unfit associate for young gentlemen of correct habits, will be punished with immediate dismission from the University.

The attendance of students upon Theatres, or similar places of amusement is strictly forbidden, and for a violation of this law it shall be the duty of the President to dismiss a student from the University.

All the students of this University are strictly required to attend public worship twice on the Sabbath, at such churches as may be designated by their parents or guardians.

Every officer will report daily at 12 o'clock, M., to the President, all the absences of every kind which he has recorded for the previous day. Once in every week, at an appointed hour, he will also report the standing of every student under his charge, with the merits and demerits of each. No officer, however, is to consider his duty fulfilled by the mere act of presenting a report. It will be his duty to see the members of his class in private, as soon as their progress in learning, or their conduct begins to be unsatisfactory, and, by all honorable motives and parental counsel, labor to cultivate in them a love of excellence and an earnest desire to improve their advantages to the utmost.

If a student is unable from ill health to pursue his studies, he shall immediately request permission of absence. Until such permission is obtained, he is held responsible for the discharge of his duties. It shall be the duty of the President immediately to communicate to the parent or guardian of a student, information that such permission of absence has been granted.

The President shall cause an accurate account to be opened with every student in a book prepared for this purpose. In it shall be entered his merit and demerit in every class which he attends, so as to present, weekly, the precise standing in all respects of every individual. This account, or the aggregate of it, shall be sent to the parent or guardian of every student, (if he be a minor,) at the close of every term.

Whenever the demerits of a student for any term amount to 30 it shall be the duty of the President to inform his parent or guardian of the fact, and whenever his demerits amount to 100 to dismiss him from the University, and to inform his parent or guardian that he has done so.

In addition to the daily and weekly reports heretofore mentioned, it shall be the duty of every Professor to make a monthly report of his labors, and the condition of his department to the Executive Board, in such manner as they shall prescribe. These various reports shall be so constructed as to furnish to the President daily and weekly a complete account of the standing and character of every student, and of the condition of the whole University, monthly, to the Executive Board.

As it is not the intention of the Corporation to provide board for the students, and as the college buildings may not be sufficient to furnish them with dormitories, each parent or guardian will be at liberty to seek for his son or ward such accommodations as he may choose, under the following regulations:—

If a student occupy a room in college, he will be required to keep it in a neat and orderly manner, to remain in it during the hours appropriated to study, to open his door at all times to an officer of instruction or discipline, and to obey all the regulations prescribed for his government, either by the Faculty or the Executive board.

No student is permitted to use camphene or any burning fluid, to keep in his room gunpowder, fire arms, or any dangerous weapon, or any intoxicating liquor, or allow of noise or any disturbance in his apartment.

Inasmuch as great inconvenience and irregularity would result from the occasional absence of students from college during term time, permission of absence, except for causes of urgent necessity, shall not be granted.

The laws of the University extend over the whole period from the commencement to the close of the term, no portion of any week being exempted from them. From 11 o'clock until evening study hours on Saturday, is allotted to exercise and recreation; but no student is allowed to leave the city during this time without permission.

It shall be the duty of every officer occupying a room in the college to take the oversight of a certain number of rooms, which he shall visit once in the day or evening, and as much oftener as he shall deem expedient, and for the good order of which he will be considered responsible; and the residence of officers in the college buildings will be arranged, and their duties so prescribed by the Faculty and Executive Board, as to give to these laws the greatest possible efficiency.

No student whose conduct is such as to give annoyance to others shall be permitted to occupy a room in the college buildings.

The President shall have authority, whenever in his opinion it becomes necessary, to direct that the funds of any student be placed in the hands of the Register; and, after this has been done, if a student receive money that is not thus accounted for, or run into debt without permission, the President is authorized to dismiss him from the University.

SECTION SEVENTH.

MISCELLANEOUS.

It shall be the duty of the Register, by advertising or otherwise, to ascertain the names of suitable persons who desire to furnish students with board and lodging, under such regulations as may be prescribed by the Executive Board. A list of such places shall be kept by him, from which parents or students may make a selection at will. No student shall board or lodge at any house which has not been thus approved, unless for special reasons, permission be given for this purpose.

Students lodging in the city are under the same regulations in respect to attendance on all the exercises required, as those in the University buildings; they are equally forbidden to leave the city without permission, or to visit any place of improper amusement. For immoral conduct they shall be liable to the same punishments as other students.

No public meetings of students shall be held except by the permission of the President.

The hours for the several courses of Lectures shall, as soon as possible, be permanently fixed by the Faculty, with the approbation of the Executive Board.

There shall be two terms in each collegiate year, the First commencing on the first Friday of September and continuing for 20 weeks, after which shall be a vacation of 4 weeks. The Second term shall commence on the fourth Friday of

February and shall continue 20 weeks, after which there shall be a vacation of 8 weeks.

The exercises of every day shall commence with prayer and the reading of the Scriptures. Absence from prayers shall incur the same demerit as from recitation.

Commencement shall be held on the 2d Wednesday of July.

Masters of Arts, Bachelors of Arts and Bachelors of Philosophy, of the two higher grades of honor, shall be entitled to Orations at Commencement. In case the number of graduates entitled to Orations be so large that the whole cannot be allowed to speak, a selection shall be made by the Faculty, from those graduates in each degree, who have most successfully cultivated the practice of Rhetoric and Oratory.

There shall be two exhibitions in each year of the class of English Literature and Rhetoric, at such time as the Faculty may appoint.

It shall be the duty of the Professor of English Literature and Rhetoric to superintend the exercises at Commencement, and the public Exhibitions, under such regulations as the Faculty may prescribe.

The Register shall have the charge of the buildings and grounds of the University; he shall receive payment for tickets to the several classes, and account for them to the proper officers; he shall employ and superintend such servants as may be required for keeping the dormitories and halls clean and in good order; he shall be an officer of discipline, residing in the college buildings, and daily reporting to the President every violation of the laws which may come within his knowledge; he shall keep all the books pertaining to the discipline of the University, under the direction of the President; collect all the dues from students to the University, and pay them to the Treasurer; he shall keep a list of the houses to which students may be recommended for board and lodging; he shall take charge of the funds of students when it is desired either by their parents or guardians, or the President, and perform such services in his department as shall be desired by the Executive Board.

It shall be the duty of the President to assign the rooms to the students residing in the University, and he shall have authority, at his discretion, to direct any student to change his room.

The price of room rent shall be fixed by the Executive Board.

Every student, when he becomes a member of the University, shall deposit with the Register a sum, to be fixed by the Executive Board, sufficient to meet his bill for a term.

www.ingramcontent.com/pod-product-compliance
Lightning Source LLC
LaVergne TN
LVHW011139110826
845150LV00008B/2414
* 9 7 8 1 4 1 8 1 9 3 6 2 1 *